The Li
M
Wyatt North

Wyatt North Publishing

© Wyatt North Publishing, LLC 2013
A Boutique Publishing Company

Publishing by Wyatt North Publishing, LLC.

Copyright © Wyatt North Publishing, LLC. All rights reserved, including the right to reproduce this book or portions thereof in any form whatsoever. For more information please visit http://www.WyattNorth.com.

Cover design by Wyatt North Publishing, LLC. Copyright © Wyatt North Publishing, LLC. All rights reserved.

Original cover artwork by Martin-loewenstein Ölbild von Żaba, Hamburg 2010. Licensed under the Creative Commons Attribution-Share Alike 3.0 Unported license.

Scripture texts in this work are taken from the *New American Bible, revised edition*© 2010, 1991, 1986, 1970 Confraternity of Christian Doctrine, Washington, D.C. and are used by permission of the copyright owner. All Rights Reserved. No part of the New American Bible may be reproduced in any form without permission in writing from the copyright owner.

About Wyatt North Publishing

Wyatt North Publishing is a boutique publishing company. We always provide high quality, perfectly formatted, Books.

We guarantee our Books. If you are not 100% satisfied we will do everything in our power to make you happy. Visit WyattNorth.com for more information. Please feel free to contact us with any questions or comments. We welcome your feedback by email at infoWyattNorth.com.

Table of Contents

About Wyatt North Publishing 3
Foreword 5
Quick Facts 6
The Life of Mother Teresa 8
    Introduction 9
    Childhood 11
    Life as a Loreto 16
    The Call Within a Call 20
    Years of Building 28
    Support and Opposition 35
    Accolades and Advancement 41
    Death 44
    Interior Life 50
    Legacy 62
Prayers by Mother Teresa 65
    Daily Prayer 66
    Nazareth Prayer for the Family 68
    Anyway 71

Foreword

One part biography, one part prayer book, The Life and Prayers of Mother Teresa is an essential for any Christian.

Mother Teresa wanted to do "something beautiful for God." At the time of her death in 1997, there were nearly 4,000 Missionaries of Charity Sisters established in 610 houses in 123 countries. The congregation did not cease growing with her death. Today, there are more than 5,000 Sisters. The work continues to thrive as the network of Missionaries of Charity continues to operate centers in countries throughout the world.

In 1985, Mother Teresa was invited to address the United Nations General Assembly. On that occasion, the Secretary General of the United Nations, Javier Pérez de Cuéllar, called her "the most powerful woman in the world."

At the end of 1999, two years after Mother Teresa's death, Gallup published a poll of America's most widely admired people of the 20th century. Mother Teresa topped the list, ahead of such luminaries as Rev. Martin Luther King, Jr., Helen Keller, Winston Churchill, and Albert Einstein.

Quick Facts

The new "Quick Facts" section in **The Life and Prayers** collection provides the reader with a collection of facts about each saint!

Born:

August 26, 1910, Skopje

Died:

September 5, 1997, Kolkata

Feast:

September 5

Beautified:

October 19, 2003, St. Peter's Basilica, Rome by Pope John Paul II

The Life of Mother Teresa

Introduction

In 1985, Mother Teresa was invited to address the United Nations General Assembly. On that occasion, the Secretary General of the United Nations, Javier Pérez de Cuéllar, called her "the most powerful woman in the world."

At the end of 1999, two years after Mother Teresa's death, Gallup published a poll of America's most widely admired people of the 20th century. Mother Teresa topped the list, ahead of such luminaries as Rev. Martin Luther King, Jr., Helen Keller, Winston Churchill, and Albert Einstein.

What was it about Mother Teresa that caused so very many people, both in America and around the globe, to revere this simple woman, and a few to revile her?

Childhood

There is no doubt that the roots of Mother Teresa's worldview stemmed from the loving family into which she was born. She entered the world on August 26, 1910, in Skopje, and was christened Gonxha ("Little Flower") Agnes Bojaxhiu the following day. Her family were ethnic Albanians, happy and prosperous. Her parents, Nikola and Dranafile (known as Drana) had come to Skopje from the Kosovan town of Prizren, probably in pursuit of better business opportunities.

Nikola was a merchant and builder, who traveled extensively on business and spoke several languages. He was a member of the town council and quite active in public life. Both Nikola and Drana modeled generous love for the poor and strove to instill this core value in their children—brother Lazar, sister Aga, and the youngest, Gonxha. The parents actively supported the poor of the community, and no one in need was ever turned away from their door. Young Gonxha frequently went with her mother on errands of mercy, bringing supplies to those in need. The family prayed together daily, and also played music together. Gonxha learned the mandolin.

At the time that Gonxha lived there, Skopje was a multiethnic city in which both Albanians and Catholics were in the minority.

This important feature of her background may account for Mother Theresa's later tolerance of non-Catholic groups. Skopje today is the capital of the Republic of Macedonia, but it lies within the troubled Balkan Peninsula and changed status numerous times in the twentieth century. During Gonxha's infancy, the city was in the process of being liberated from five hundred years of Ottoman control. It was annexed by the Kingdom of Serbia in 1912, shortly before Albania declared independence along the Serbian border. Following W.W.I, it became part of the new Kingdom of Yugoslavia.

Although Skopje was away from the main centers of upheaval, the regional troubles eventually came home to roost for the Bojaxhiu family. Gonxha's father, Nikola, was an ardent Albanian nationalist and actively involved in nationalist causes. Key figures of the Albanian resistance frequently met in the family home. In 1919, Nikola journeyed to Belgrade for an activists' meeting and returned home acutely ill. Although only forty-five and normally in vigorous health, he died a day later. The family believed he had been poisoned by political enemies. Gonxha was only eight at the time.

Now the fortunes of the family changed. Nikola's business partners abandoned his young widow, leaving the family with little more than their home. The grief-stricken Drana was forced to become the family breadwinner. She began a business dealing in needlework, cloth, and carpets. Despite their own strained finances, the devoutly religious Drana continued to feed and assist those in even worse circumstances. In later years, Mother Teresa especially remembered an alcoholic woman, abandoned by her family, whose bodily sores her mother lovingly tended. She often recalled that the worst suffering this woman experienced was her loneliness. There is no question that the model of her parents, and especially Drana, helped guide Gonxha to her vocation.

During this difficult time, the Church provided emotional and spiritual support to the Bojaxhiu family. The family regularly attended the parish church of the Sacred Heart, where Gonxha and Aga were featured singers in the church choir. They made annual pilgrimages to the nearby Madonna of the Black Mountain at Letnice, whom Mother Teresa later credited with helping decide her vocation. She felt a calling to be a missionary as early as the age of twelve, although the desire to become a nun came later.

Beginning in 1925, the parish priest was a Jesuit named Father Jambrekovic, who had a notable talent for engaging his young parishioners. Gonxha was an active member of the mixed youth group, which went on outings, but she was especially influenced by the girls' group, the Sodality of Children of Mary, where she became acquainted with the Spiritual Exercises of St. Ignatius of Loyola directing her to make room for Jesus in her life. She also read deeply from the church library. Father Jambrekovic enthusiastically kept his parishioners informed about the work of Jesuit missions, particularly those in India. Gonxha was fascinated, and she was particularly drawn by accounts about the Loreto Sisters in India. By the age of eighteen, she had decided to joint them.

Life as a Loreto

The Loreto Sisters, more formally known as The Institute of the Blessed Virgin Mary, were founded by Mary Ward, an English woman, in 1609. Mary Ward envisioned a self-governing congregation patterned after the Jesuits, intellectual and active in the world beyond the cloister. The group that Gonxha would join was based in Ireland. Drana gave her consent on condition that Gonxha give herself completely to God. This condition followed Gonxha throughout her life as she tried to live up to her mother's terms. Her soldier brother Lazar was more skeptical. Gonxha replied to him: "You think you are important because you are an officer serving a king with two million subjects. But I am serving the King of the whole world." (Forty years later, Lazar would be present in Norway to witness her receiving the Nobel Prize.)

And so with Drana and Aga to accompany her, Gonxha set off by train to Zagreb in September 1928. She waited in Zagreb for another prospective postulant to join her and then, in October, bade farewell to her mother and sister to travel by train across Europe. She would never see them again. The two candidates were interviewed in Paris and allowed to continue on to the motherhouse in Dublin, where they officially became postulants. They spent six weeks at the motherhouse studying English, and

Gonxha chose the name Sister Mary Teresa, after Therese of Lisieux, the Little Flower.

In December, they set sail for India. A month later, Sister Teresa had her first contact with India, where the level of poverty initially shocked her. She travelled from Madras to Calcutta and on to Darjeeling, which was approximately 400 miles north of Calcutta in the foothills of the Himalayas. There, in May 1929, she received her habit and became a novice. As part of her novitiate, she studied Hindi and Bengali in preparation for her teaching mission. Her first teaching experience was in the Loreto school in Darjeeling, and she also assisted in a clinic, where she first became aware of the horrific medical issues brought by extreme poverty.

Having taken her initial vows, Sister Teresa was next sent to the Loreto Entally community in Calcutta (today called Kolkata). She would spend nearly two decades there, happily engaged with meaningful work. She wrote of the joy she found in imitating Jesus' earthly work and observing his command to teach the nations (Matthew 28:19-20). The approach of the Loreto Sisters was to overcome poverty through education. Accordingly, Sister Teresa taught geography and history in the St. Mary's Bengali Medium School for girls. The lessons were given in Bengali. In May 1937, Sister Teresa took her final vows of poverty, chastity, and obedience, and would henceforth be known as Mother Teresa, which was customary among the Loreto's. Even at this early stage in her career, she would go out to visit the poor on Sundays, bringing them what joy she could.

The years of the Second World War brought a great many challenges. St. Mary's School was requisitioned by the British for military use, and other quarters had to be found for the school. During those difficult years, Mother Teresa became known for her resourcefulness. In fact, her efforts were nothing short of heroic. She helped her students survive the catastrophic Bengal famine of 1942-43. In 1944, she became principal of the school and the superior of the Daughters of St. Anne (the Bengali Sisters affiliated with Loreto). When Hindu-Muslim violence broke out in 1946, resulting in tremendous loss of life in Calcutta, Mother Teresa ventured out to seek food for her 300 charges. Having witnessed the carnage, she successfully returned with bags of rice.

The Call Within a Call

Mother Teresa truly loved her time as a Loreto Sister, and

she would say in later years that leaving the order was the most difficult thing she had to do in her life. Nevertheless, the poverty that surrounded her in Calcutta pulled her and made her wonder if there wasn't something more she could do. The answer came in September 1946, when she took a train trip back to Darjeeling on retreat. She referred to what happened on that trip as "the call within a call," but during her lifetime would never reveal the details of what had occurred. She simply stated that she had never had a vision.

Only after her death did details about what had occurred emerge from her private correspondence. For a time during the years 1946–47, Mother Teresa experienced a period of intense closeness to God. She heard, through interior speech, Jesus calling her to bring him to the poor and thereby satisfy his thirst for souls and comfort his suffering heart. She thus felt called to go out to minister directly to "the poorest of the poor." The personal cost for her was leaving the comfort and fellowship of Loreto.

As it happened, it would be nearly two years before she received permission to follow the call. She petitioned repeatedly during that time, but it was only in 1948, nineteen years after her arrival in India, that she received permission to leave Loreto for up to one year with an indult of exclaustration, which meant that she was to keep her religious vows when she left. After that year, the Archbishop of Calcutta would need to review her situation. Over her objections, the door was left open to her to return to Loreto. She did not feel the open door was necessary: God would see to it that she succeeded.

The indult had been signed in April but only reached Calcutta in August, and it was on August 17, 1948, that she finally left Loreto with a mere five rupees. No longer wearing the black habit of the Loreto Sisters, she now wore a white habit and a white sari with blue-striped edging, which she had purchased because it was simple and inexpensive.

She traveled by train to Patna for a brief period of training with the Medical Mission Sisters at Holy Family Hospital. When she returned to Calcutta, it was with the clear intention of beginning a new congregation that would reside among the poorest of India's inhabitants, living as they did and tending to their needs. In order to bring the people of India to Christ, she would become Indian. Indeed, she even obtained Indian citizenship. India had achieved independence barely a year before.

Initially, Mother Teresa lived with the Little Sisters of the Poor. Beginning in December 1948, she went daily into the slums to see what service she could render. She very quickly established an outdoor school. The ground and a stick were her blackboard and chalk. She taught the destitute children the alphabet, hygiene, catechism, and needlework, followed by visits to the sick. In one encounter, she came across a woman dying outside a hospital. The hospital had refused to admit the woman because she was indigent, so she died on the ground outside. Experiences like these convinced Mother Teresa of the need for a place where destitute sick people could come to die with dignity.

As time passed, word spread about Mother Teresa's work and small donations began to come in. She was able to rent two hovels: one became a school building, the other a shelter for the sick and dying. She was also granted space within a Christian home, and this became an incipient convent as some of her former students from the Loreto Entally school began to join her, one at a time. With considerable priestly assistance, constitutions for the new congregation were drawn up, and accepted by Pope Pius XII in 1950. (These were later revised in accordance with the guidelines of Vatican II.) The new congregation of the Missionary Sisters of Charity was now official, and the eleven young women who had by then joined Mother Teresa formally became postulants. Their four vows would be fidelity to poverty, chastity, obedience, and wholehearted and free service to the poorest of the poor.

A Life of Material Poverty

Mother Teresa was determined from the very beginning that her new congregation would never adopt a lifestyle of comfort or ease. In order to minister to the poor with the level of love and good humor she required, her Sisters would need to understand the poor. The best way to achieve this was to be poor themselves. She was conscious that the people she served had no choice in their poverty, even though the Sisters did.

Originally, she had wanted the diet they adopted to consist of only the rice and salt eaten by the poor of India. She was persuaded by other nuns working among the poor that to maintain the strength needed for their work and not become sick themselves, they would have to eat a bit better than that. As a result, the diet was nominally improved, but she was also careful to make sure the Sisters took vitamins and had periods of rest.

On the whole, the Sisters lived very meagerly. They were to own very little besides their garments and the umbrella necessary for a bit of protection against the monsoon rains. The sisters washed their few garments by hand in buckets. Even later, when donations came more readily, she refused donations of conveniences like washing machines or fans for the convent, always believing in the importance of living as the poor did. Whatever donations did come were to go to the poor, not to enhance the comfort of the Sisters.

Mother Teresa always emphasized humility in service. Beginning in 1967, she asked her Sisters to say a morning prayer prior to embarking upon their work in the world. The prayer began, "Make us worthy, Lord, to serve our fellow men throughout the world who live and die in poverty and hunger." Helping the marginalized people in society made one merely a humble tool for God's actions. It wasn't intended to be a source of pride.

The order was to depend upon Providence for its own subsistence and for whatever materials or food they needed to help others. Providence did not disappoint them: time and again, supplies arrived just when they were needed most. Mother Teresa and the other Sisters also became adept at begging door to door. Their long days were filled with prayer, learning, spiritual contemplation, and most of all, productive work. Although their lives were materially poor, they were spiritually rich.

Years of Building

The Missionary Sisters of Charity soon outgrew their original quarters in the Christian residence, and in early 1953 moved to a centrally located property purchased from one of the many Indian Muslims relocating to Pakistan in those days. Because the elderly man had been educated by Jesuits, he generously agreed to sell the property to the Sisters for far less than its value. This location is still the motherhouse of the order today.

In the years following Partition, India was flooded with refugees from Pakistan. International relief efforts were woefully inadequate. The numbers of starving and dying people on the streets of Calcutta reached such a high level that the municipal government finally felt compelled to do something. When Mother Teresa petitioned for a building to use as a shelter for the dying, the city granted her a disused pilgrim hostel attached to the Hindu Temple of Kali. This facility became her home for the dying, Nirmal Hriday ("Pure Heart," in honor of the Immaculate Heart), where the abandoned were no longer alone—they could die with caring attention, surrounded by love. The policy for admission was strikingly tolerant: people of any faith were accepted, and they were able to receive whatever death rites and comfort were appropriate to their various religions.

The problem of unwanted children, many disabled, was also acute in Calcutta. Mother Teresa was always especially tender with young children, believing that every child—whatever its condition or disability—was a gift from God. In September 1955, the Missionaries of Charity opened its first children's home, located near the motherhouse. A certain number of the children and babies found by the Sisters or brought to them died. Others could be nursed back to health and were either restored to their parents or entered the long-term care of the Missionaries of Charity. At Shishu Bhavan, efforts were made to provide the most capable children with an education, and others with a trade of some sort so that they would eventually be self-sustaining. Private sponsors were sought to pay for the tuition of individual children at Indian schools. (By 1975, this approach had become too unwieldy, and a general fund for education was established, the World Child Welfare Fund.)

Leprosy, or Hansen's disease, quickly became another focus for Mother Teresa's work. Today it is considered curable: the World Health Organization has a global campaign to eliminate leprosy and has been making free multidrug treatment available since 1995. The multidrug approach was first adopted in 1981. The disease, however, continues to be a problem among the poor, particularly in India, where it originated. When Mother Teresa first began her work with lepers, the disease was endemic in India, and only one drug was available for its treatment.

The worst part of leprosy has always been the social stigma and isolation that befall its victims. Mother Teresa wanted those afflicted with leprosy to know that they, too, were children of God. She wanted them to want to live. Consequently, Mother Teresa's approach was two-pronged: to alleviate the isolation and to make treatment available. Her collection boxes for the cause pointedly proclaimed: "Touch a leper with your compassion." Beginning in 1957, she established mobile leprosy clinics to bring medicine to the areas where the afflicted lived. This meant that they could remain with their families. She also opened centers where patients needing prolonged treatment could be helped. In the 1960s, on land provided by the Indian government, she opened Shanti Nagar, "Place of Peace," a village with food production and trades, where people with leprosy could live purposeful lives.

By the end of the 1950s, the reputation of the Missionary Sisters of Charity was spreading. Other cities in India welcomed their efforts: a children's home was opened in Delhi and a home for the dying in Bombay (Mumbai). Their outreach grew to encompass whatever specific need they saw, whether prenatal care, tuberculosis treatment, vocational training, or relief from natural disasters like flood or earthquake.

Then, in 1965, came an important new step: an invitation to open a mission outside of India in Venezuela. The needs in Venezuela were far different than those in India, but the Sisters followed their policy of doing what the poor needed. In Venezuela, the poor were lapsed Catholics living with a shortage of religious functionaries to guide them. In addition to their usual tasks of tending the poor and sick, the Sisters undertook to educate the children in Catholicism and provide such religious services as they were able, some of them even receiving the authority in 1970 to administer Communion.

Invitations next followed from Rome, Tanzania, Australia, and a host of other locations, each with its own challenges. In 1979, she was able to open the first foundation in a Communist country in Zagreb, which at the time was part of Yugoslavia. The Communist countries (and formerly Communist countries) would always hold particular interest for her. In Western countries, what shocked Mother Teresa was the spiritual poverty amidst plenty. Drug and alcohol abuse, prostitution, abandonment of the elderly and mentally ill—these were the issues they confronted in materially rich societies.

Whenever a new site was being established, Mother Teresa would travel there with a handful of Sisters to make sure that a good start was made. She had to learn to delegate authority to the new superiors of each site, but she was careful always to ensure that the mission would faithfully represent the principles she had set forth. In each location, it was vital that poverty be maintained, service be cheerful, and work be performed out of love. Visiting the growing number of missions around the world would consume an increasing amount of her time.

As the congregation of Sisters was growing and thriving, Mother Teresa began to see the value of starting a congregation of Brothers. In 1963, she began a society of Brothers, which eventually came under the authority of Brother Andrew, a former Jesuit from Australia who had been deeply affected by Mother Teresa and decided to join her work. The Missionary Brothers of Charity was recognized by the Church as a congregation in 1967. During the 1970s, the Brothers established houses in such disparate places as Los Angeles and Hong Kong. While remaining essentially true to the vision of Mother Teresa, they have also forged their own path.

Mother Teresa's efforts were continually expanding. In 1976, she founded a new branch of the Sisters, which came to be known as the Missionaries of Charity, Contemplative. This group would devote several hours a day to working with the poor, but the majority of each day would be spent in contemplative prayer. The Sisters' chapel would be open to anyone from outside seeking a quiet respite. Mother Teresa later established a parallel contemplative branch of Brothers (1979). The Corpus Christi Movement, established in 1981, allowed diocesan priests to share in the work. Eventually, with the help of Father Joseph Langford (d. 2010) of the United States, a separate congregation for priests was also established, the Missionaries of Charity Fathers (1984), which began with the express blessing of Pope John Paul II.

In 1985, the crisis of AIDS was brought to Mother Teresa's attention by a letter she received. She saw the stark parallel between the treatment of people with AIDS and the lepers she had been accustomed to helping: both were societal outcasts often rejected by their own families. The same year, she opened the Gift of Love in New York City. She called it a birthday gift for Jesus because it was opened on Christmas Eve. It would be the first of several residences for patients dying of AIDS. At a time when there was still no effective treatment for AIDS, she counseled the path of love, rather than judgment or fear.

Support and Opposition

The work did not always advance smoothly. Groups both within and without Indian society have at different times been suspicious and hostile towards Mother Teresa's efforts. Orthodox Hindus, for example, were initially opposed to the location of a home for the dying so close to the Temple of Kali, since corpses were viewed as impure. Other Indians feared attempts to convert Hindus, although overt conversion efforts were never part of Mother Teresa's approach. She always felt that an example of love was the best way to win converts. (Christians remain only a very small percentage of the city's population, less than 1%.)

More serious were the criticisms of unsanitary conditions at her facilities: the Sisters and volunteers touched those they were tending without gloves. This was because of Mother Teresa's central tenet that suffering people represent the suffering Christ: to touch them is to touch Christ. Consequently, gloves were seen as an unwanted form of distancing a caretaker from that goal. Nevertheless, this approach carried the risk of spreading disease among both the caretakers and the inmates. There were also accusations of reuse of needles and failure to alleviate pain.

Social activists over the years have criticized Mother Teresa for dealing with dictators and for not addressing the underlying causes of poverty, which she did not view as her mission. Her mission, as she saw it, was to minister to the needs of individuals. Others could fight for social justice, but while they were doing it, the poor were dying. Her task was to apply herself to people's immediate needs for food, shelter, and love.

Activists within the Church, too, were often disappointed by her traditional stances. She remained particularly traditional in her attitude toward the role of women. Women should be homemakers, she felt. After all, fracturing of the family was in many ways responsible for the breakdown and spiritual poverty of Western society. She often blamed the Western spiritual malaise on the failure of families to pray together and to love one another enough. She told her Co-Workers to first make sure that the needs of their family members were met: "Bring love into your home. If you really love God, begin by loving your child, your husband, your wife." Even before starting her congregation, she envisioned it as especially working for the "unity and happiness of family life" (Letter to Archbishop Perier). Accordingly, she was outspoken in her opposition to abortion, which she viewed as the greatest destroyer of peace. She was also opposed to the idea of women becoming priests and bristled at religious figures who dressed in street clothes. One former

Sister accused her of infantilizing the Sisters by restricting their reading material (no secular materials, including newspapers, are allowed) and discouraging individual initiative.

There were also setbacks along the way. A few of the first Sisters left the order. Several others died in tragic circumstances while ministering to the poor. For a time, there was hurtful resentment from some of her former colleagues at the Loreto Entally school, who were displeased at the number of girls who were joining her. On rare occasions, they were forced to abandon missions. The Brothers' mission in Vietnam was shut down by the Communist government, and the Sisters found they were unwanted in Belfast. In later years, centers for AIDS patients faced opposition from the community, particularly the Gift of Peace in Washington, D.C. Perhaps worst of all, in 1980, a fire broke out in the women's shelter in London, killing ten residents and a volunteer. Yet another horrible incident occurred in 1986 when Mother Teresa's plane was taking off in Tanzania and spun into a crowd of well-wishers who had come to bid her farewell. Five people were killed, including three children and a Sister. Towards the end of Mother Teresa's life, in 1996, both the superior and the regional superior for New York were killed in an automobile accident. Such sorrowful events caused Mother Teresa heartache but did not stop her work.

There were private troubles as well. Communication with her mother was painfully sporadic because of Communist rule where her mother and sister resided. A letter might get through once in a decade. In July 1972, Drana died, followed only a year later by Aga. Mother Teresa had never been able to return to see them because the existing regime refused to offer guarantees that it wouldn't prevent her leaving the country again.

Meanwhile, however, Mother Teresa was accumulating important supporters, including volunteer doctors and nurses, wealthy Hindu and Muslim donors, powerful members of the Indian government, and eventually global heads of state. Volunteers and Sisters alike often found the work indescribably rewarding. Her work among the poor of India was increasingly appreciated by people at all levels of Indian society. She was afforded free travel on Indian Railways, and Indira Gandhi herself provided Mother Teresa with a free pass on Indian Airways so that she could travel to the congregation's other locations.

Her support was strikingly non-denominational. In fact, the language of the constitution of the International Association of Co-Workers of Mother Teresa, which was formally organized in 1969 (although it had existed informally for quite some time before that), was pointedly sensitive to the diversity of people who wanted to support her work. The organization was constituted for people of all ages and "all religions and denominations throughout the world who seek to love God in their fellow men through wholehearted free service to the poorest of the poor of all castes and creeds…" She was pleased that she counted among her supporters Hindus, Muslims, Parsees, Jews, Buddhists, and Protestants, in addition to Catholics.

The tasks undertaken by the Co-Workers varied, depending upon location and need. Mother Teresa advised her Co-Workers first to look around at the needs that were close by to them. Were there neighbors who could use their help in some small way? Were there lonely people who would appreciate a visit? In some cases, the Co-Workers worked side-by-side with the Sisters as volunteers. In other cases, they might run a resale shop or raise money in other ways. They could also help with their prayers and spiritual support, which Mother Teresa viewed as being vital to the ongoing success of the work. Mother Teresa was adamant, however, that the group not become merely a fund-raising organization, and she was careful that organizational infrastructure did not eat up funds earmarked for the needy. Within a decade, the group would have nearly 800,000 members.

Accolades and Advancement

Papal support of the Missionary Sisters of Charity became official under Pope Paul VI in 1965, when the congregation was accorded the Decree of Praise by the Sacred Council for the Propagation of the Faith. As her congregation grew, more Vatican recognition would follow. In 1971, she was awarded the first Pope John XXIII Peace Prize. In 1975, she was named a member of the Vatican delegation to the International Women's Year World Conference. In 1980, she addressed the World Synod of Bishops, which was gathered in Rome, on the subject of the Christian family.

Mother Teresa's international acclaim began as early as 1962, when she received the Magsaysay Prize for International Understanding, which is awarded in commemoration of a beloved Philippine president who died in a plane crash. She received several awards from the Indian government, including the Padma Shri (1962), and the Nehru Award (1972), and the Bharat Ratna (India's highest civilian award; 1980). In 1973, she was the first recipient of the Templeton Prize for Progress in Religion. As her reputation grew, prestigious awards followed in quick succession as organizations and institutions everywhere vied for her attention. These honors culminated with her 1979 receipt of the Nobel Peace Prize.

Even at these elegant occasions, Mother Teresa maintained her commitment to a life of poverty. She would decline all food and drink, accepting only a glass of water for refreshment. She had early established a rule forbidding Sisters to accept food outside the convent. This was so that they would not need to take food from a poor person if it was offered as a gesture of hospitality.

Actually, Mother Teresa's initial response to early publicity was one of fear. She was concerned it would challenge her humility and distract her from the work. She only accepted the growing number of honors because they afforded her the opportunity to spread her message, which was, she felt, God's own message. She did not like public speaking and never prepared a formal speech for these events. Instead, she would pray beforehand and then speak extemporaneously in the name of "the poor, the hungry, the sick, and the lonely." Sometimes, as when she received the Nobel Prize, she used the occasion as a platform to speak against abortion. Any monetary awards that accompanied the prizes went to advance her work with the poor.

Death

The indefatigable stamina with which Mother Teresa pursued her work is all the more astonishing in light of her medical history. As a child she was susceptible to respiratory ailments. Later, as a Loreto, she was placed on enforced bed rest for a period of time and then sent on retreat to Darjeeling to recoup her strength. (It was while traveling there that she received her "call within a call.") Over the years she suffered from malaria, which would recur from time to time. And, while blessed with long life, she experienced the health decline of advancing age. Her eyes began to worsen, and she suffered from inflamed vertebrae (spondylitis), which shortened and bent her already diminutive stature. In 1974, she had a slight stroke, and in 1981—the year in which she celebrated the fiftieth anniversary of her religious vows—she was diagnosed with a severe heart condition.

In 1989, she was hospitalized for a number of weeks for her heart condition, which had been aggravated by her malaria, and eventually she received a pacemaker. In 1991, she came down with bacterial pneumonia while visiting the United States and Mexico, and she underwent angioplasty while hospitalized. Other hospitalizations would follow in the time remaining to her, and there were several falls as well.

Mother Teresa viewed any physical trials she had to undergo as helpful to her work because she dedicated it as a sacrifice to the cause. She did not fear death. As a person of faith, she viewed it as going home to God. She joked that in one of her health crises she had gone to heaven but that St. Peter had sent her back to earth because there were no slums in heaven.

At least as early as 1979, she had been trying to relinquish her administrative leadership of the Missionaries of Charity, feeling that someone younger might be more suitable. Nevertheless, against her own wishes, she was unanimously reelected superior general at every chapter general meeting. The only dissenting vote was consistently her own. Finally, in 1990, she tended her resignation to Pope John Paul II, who accepted it. The Sisters, however, did not, and once again she was reelected to leadership.

Although her declining health caused Mother Teresa to rely on others for administrative help, her world travels continued. In her final years, she was still able to accomplish some important projects. In 1991, she was finally able to open a house in Albania, and in 1992, following Operation Desert Storm, she was permitted to open a house in Iraq. The one goal that eluded her was opening a home in China, although she did manage to make two visits there, which helped to ease tensions with the Vatican.

As Mother Teresa aged, so did many of those who had shared her journey. She lost some of her closest companions. For many years, Sister Agnes was the heir presumptive to Mother Teresa. She had been Mother Teresa's very first companion and had assisted Mother Teresa in so many ways over the years, but she was diagnosed with cancer in 1990 and died in April 1997. Father Celeste Van Exem, the Belgian Jesuit who had been Mother Teresa's spiritual advisor for many years and had helped her first organize the Missionaries of Charity, died in September 1993. He had offered God his life in exchange for Mother Teresa's. And Ann Blaikie, another early companion and the driving force behind the Co-Workers, died in January 1996.

At times Mother Teresa suffered lapses of memory. Heart, lung, and renal failure were increasingly taking their toll. In August 1996, she was placed on a respirator but then rallied. September 10, 1996, was the fiftieth anniversary of Inspiration Day, her "call within a call." She spent the day in quiet reflection.

By now, it was clear that the mostly bed-ridden Mother Teresa could no longer continue her duties, but the Missionaries of Charity Sisters had a difficult time reconciling to that reality.

Finally, in March 1997, a successor was elected, Sister Nirmala Joshi, who had been head of the Contemplative Sisters. Mother Teresa was well pleased with the choice. Sister Nirmala was a Hindu convert whose parents had come to India from Nepal. Sweet-faced and highly educated, she asked for prayers so that the Lord would make her worthy. She declined the title of Mother, in deference to Mother Teresa. In the view of the Sisters, there could be only one "Mother." (Sister Nirmala's term as Superior General was completed in 2009. She was succeeded by the German-born Sister Mary Prema Pierick, who had been regional head of the European Sisters.)

Mother Teresa managed a final trip to Rome to present Sister Nirmala to the Pope, and to the United States, where she received a Congressional Gold Medal. While in New York, she had met with Princess Diana, a long-time acquaintance. The death of Diana on August 31, 1997, occasioned Mother Teresa's last public statement in which she said that she would pray for her friend.

On September 5, 1997, at 9:30 PM, Mother Teresa died at the motherhouse in Calcutta. Her body was transferred to St. Thomas's Church, located next to the Loreto convent, so that larger numbers of people could come to honor her. On September 13, she was accorded a state funeral by the government of India. Her body was carried through the streets of Calcutta on the same gun carriage that had borne the bodies of Gandhi and Nehru. Crowds of many thousands lined the streets to bid farewell to "Ma." Heads of state and people of international prestige were present to pay their respects, signifying the nearly universal esteem in which she was held. Thereafter, Mother Teresa was laid to rest in the motherhouse in a private ceremony.

Interior Life

Mother Teresa did not like to dwell on the details of her own life except insofar as those details shone light on a moral lesson. She was especially reticent about her own interior religious experience and repeatedly asked that correspondence to her spiritual advisors be destroyed. She felt that any details about her deflected attention from God, who was the source of anything she accomplished and the proper focus of people's attentions. She was, after all, merely a "pencil in God's hand," a tool for enacting God's will in the world. All her success was due to him. Others, however, felt differently. Minimally, the documents were seen as important for recording the history of the Missionaries of Charity. Perhaps more importantly, they were vital for understanding the life of a woman who might just possibly be a saint. Mother Teresa did destroy some documents, but others were preserved and published after her death.

Surprisingly, what emerged from her correspondence was that Mother Teresa's experience of God wasn't uniform. Despite her resolutely cheerful countenance, she underwent long years of doubt to match the depth of her faith. This information makes her less unreachable to the rest of us and is worth exploring.

Even while preparing to take her final vows as a Loreto, she wrote to Father Jambrekovic of Skopje that darkness was often her companion, but she countered it by carrying her cross with great joy. When darkness did come to her, she overcame it by surrendering herself to Jesus. She readily embraced her trials as a way to share in Jesus' suffering and to show her great love for him.

In April 1942, several years after making her final profession as a Loreto, she made a private vow not to refuse anything God asked of her. This was Mother Teresa's freewill gift of love for Jesus. The vow was intended as an expression of her complete devotion and desire for closeness to the divine. She was fully ready to subsume her own will entirely to God's will. As a result of the vow, she developed her characteristic tendency to haste, born not of impetuousness, but out of the desire to act quickly and with resolve once she had determined God's will. Commitment to her vow would propel her towards her future role as founder of the Missionaries of Charity.

Mother Teresa was thirty-six years old when she received her "call within a call." It was September 10, 1946—Inspiration Day—the date Mother Teresa considered to be the beginning of the Missionaries of Charity. On that date, while travelling in the train to her retreat in Darjeeling, Jesus invited her to "come be my light." She was called to give up everything and follow Jesus into the slums to serve the poorest of the poor. Her viewpoint from the beginning was rooted in the message that Jesus was thirsty for souls and was calling her to quench his thirst. That, in fact, is the express purpose of the Missionaries of Charity, as articulated in its Rules: to satiate the thirst of Jesus Christ on the cross. In every Missionaries of Charity convent, the words "I Thirst" (John 19:28) adorn the wall of the chapel, next to the crucifix. These words serve as a constant reminder of the congregation's mission. Her aim was to make God's love known to the poor and suffering, and thereby illuminate their lives and bring joy to their homes. The converse side of this activity would be to bring joy to Jesus' own heart.

Beginning on September 10 and continuing through part of the following year, Mother Teresa received "interior locutions," divine messages that came to her as speech within. The position of the Catholic Church is that Jesus spoke to her directly, asking her to undertake his work. Mother Teresa referred to his words as "the Voice," or the voice in her heart. Thus began an intimate dialogue between Jesus and his "little one." Mother Teresa also experienced at least three imaginative visions in which she saw great crowds of people. In these visions, either Jesus, the Holy Mother, or the crowd itself would implore her to go to the people and save them.

Mother Teresa grappled with doubts about her ability to fulfill this mission. She feared taking on the impoverished lifestyle of an Indian and was concerned that she would be ridiculed. She asked Jesus if she couldn't instead be a wholehearted victim for him as a Loreto. She was also prepared to accept the rejection of her superiors if they told her to abandon her plans; obedience was her byword. But the compulsion remained, and Jesus' rejoinder kept coming to her, "Wilt thou refuse?"

When Mother Teresa returned to Calcutta in October, she quickly shared her experience with Father Van Exem, her spiritual advisor at the time. Father Van Exem tested the authenticity of her message by requiring a certain passage of time before acting. She was advised to pray and remain silent on the subject. If the message were genuine, it would persist.

During this time of delay, Mother Teresa met extensively with Father Van Exem, and their frequent meetings occasioned concern among some of the Loreto Sisters, who at this point knew nothing about Mother Teresa's call or the urgent need for her meetings with Father Van Exem. As a result of this misunderstanding, Mother Teresa was transferred to the Loreto community at Asansol, about 140 miles distant from Calcutta, where she again taught Hindi and Bengali, Hygiene, and

Geography, but also had more free time in which to pray, reflect, and consider her plans. She accepted her transfer with complete equanimity, but over time the wait became distressing. She was now convinced of her calling and wanted to act.

Eventually, Mother Teresa and Father Van Exam shared the news with Archbishop Perier (also a Jesuit), who felt he needed time to pray, consider the matter, and await guidance from the Holy Spirit. He also sought the advice of Rome. She tried his patience by writing to him repeatedly, exhorting him to act quickly because souls were waiting. He, in turn, was more prosaic, asking her for a concrete plan of action, including details of recruitment and training for the new group she was proposing. He did not understand her haste because he did not know about her earlier private vow. Among the other issues he raised with her was whether the work she described could be undertaken by an existing congregation or through the creation of a lay association rather than a new congregation.

On the very letter she had received from Archbishop Perier, Mother Teresa wrote down a prayer asking that her personal limitations not prevent her from formulating suitable answers to his questions. She saw herself as unworthy of being tasked with her mission but selected by God for precisely that reason. She was again setting forth for a retreat in Darjeeling and planned to write her answers to Archbishop Perier there. While on retreat, Mother Teresa experienced an onslaught of doubt for five days, followed by renewed certainty. She was able to put practical plans into writing in response to Archbishop Perier's questions.

In July 1947, believing that the suspicions against Mother Teresa had been unjust, the Loreto superior general intervened and returned Mother Teresa to Calcutta. After her return, Jesus told Mother Teresa that her purpose for returning to Calcutta was to prepare for her mission by learning from Father Van Exem, who would communicate the divine will to her.

Father Van Exem, for his part, was highly impressed with Mother Teresa's virtue and devotion to God. He believed that God had raised her to a higher level of prayer and that the next step in her spiritual selection might be to enter a mystical state of ecstasy. He expressed to Archbishop Perier his concern that he himself might not be ready for her to take that next step. Archbishop Perier, on the other hand, remained unconvinced. He was not particularly impressed with the extra-normal activity and was uncertain whether Mother Teresa's call was self-willed. Father Van Exem assured the archbishop that neither he nor Mother Teresa considered the interior locutions and visions central to her calling or the reason for its authenticity.

For Father Van Exem, it was Mother Teresa's extraordinary virtue, ability, preparatory trials, and depth of grace that had convinced him. For Mother Teresa, the call could not have been self-willed because she had nothing on a material level to gain from it. She was already so happy at Loreto, where she was accomplishing her reasons for coming to India. Following this new call could only pose hardship and the loss of much that had been meaningful to her. She wrote to the archbishop about how she had learned self-abnegation and was eager to be wholly consumed as a victim for Christ.

Finally, Archbishop Perier reached a decision. In January 1948, he gave his approval because he believed her capable of addressing a real need of the Church. Through her, God would be able to do his work. She still needed the permission of the Loreto superior general in Dublin and the Sacred Congregation for the Religious in Rome. Now Archbishop Perier became her champion and helped her through the remainder of the process. It was only at this point that anyone at Loreto became aware of her plans, and she did not mention her interior locutions. When the time came, she left Loreto and set out for Patna full of fear, but also full of trust in God. Jesus, after all, had promised never to leave her. When she returned to Calcutta, she went into a retreat for eight days and then began her work.

Initially, during the time that the indult of exclaustration was in effect, she was sometimes tempted to return to the ease of Loreto. The transition was hard and the loneliness severe. She missed her friends at Loreto. Sometimes even her resolve to be outwardly cheerful faltered. She kept to her difficult course due to love of God, adapting to a new way of life and confronting a new type of work. The loneliness eased somewhat as future Sisters gradually came to join her.

Meanwhile, her inner life was also undergoing a severe change. The period of intense closeness to God that characterized Mother Teresa's "call within the call" was followed by a lengthy period of aridity during which she suffered a feeling of renewed distance from God. For the rest of her life, from the time that she left Loreto and began her work, she experienced varying degrees of interior darkness. She didn't reveal this aspect of her struggle to anyone until after the move to the new motherhouse in 1953, when she disclosed it in a letter to Archbishop Perier. Shortly thereafter, she took her final vows as a Missionary of Charity, and the first ten young women who had joined her took their first vows. This step brought her profound gratitude, which she often felt as her work grew. Archbishop Perier reminded her that God was present in the success of her work. Still, her loneliness for Jesus did not diminish.

Reflecting upon this turn of events, she initially feared that she might have taken a wrong turn on the path laid out for her. She wondered whether it was due to her own sinfulness being in need of purification. It became hard to pray or even to believe. In her faith and her doubt, she told Jesus that she was ready to suffer this abjectness for all eternity if it was his will and would save even one soul. Sometimes she asked for her darkness to lighten, but at the same time she prayed for the strength to bear it willingly as a sacrifice for Jesus. She felt empty of God, but at the same time she longed unrelentingly for him. The contradictions of her life tormented her. She did not want to be a hypocrite.

It was vital to Mother Teresa that she continue to smile for Jesus, for the Sisters, for the poor. The goal of the Missionaries of Charity was to "comfort [rather] than to be comforted…to love rather than be loved." She could not spread joy and comfort if her inner distress showed on her face. Consequently, she viewed her smile as a necessary "cloak" to cover her pain.

Only gradually did her spiritual advisors, particularly Father Joseph Neuner, help her to realize that this sense of isolation was part of her mission. In order to be close to the people she served, she had taken on their life of material poverty. Now, she came to understand, she was also being called to experience their darkness of the spirit. Jesus, too, had experienced that feeling of isolation and abandonment when he cried out to God from the cross (Mark 15:34). Mother Teresa's mission included sharing that part of Jesus' suffering, that sharing in the woe of a benighted humanity. Her pain was Jesus' pain. She thirsted just as Jesus thirsted. She told Father Neuner that with his help she had come for the first time to love the darkness. Her smile need no longer be a cloak. The darkness and pain did not lessen, but now there was consolation and acceptance through deepened understanding.

When her correspondence became known, many were dismayed to learn that Mother Teresa had harbored doubts; and, unfortunately, some people have willfully sensationalized her so-called dark side. It is both remarkable and highly significant that she was able to continue her labors despite the personal agony occasioned by this void. The Catholic Church views valorous struggle against spiritual darkness frequently to be part of the experience of a saint. It has been documented by such spiritual giants as St. John of the Cross, a fact that her spiritual advisors did not hesitate to point out to her.

Although she missed the interior experience of God, there is little question that Mother Teresa found God in her work. She saw Jesus constantly in the face of the suffering: "As you did it to one of the least of these my brethren, you did it to me" (Matthew 25:40). In this way, she brought comfort, and even joy, to Jesus.

It is also important to remember that Mother Teresa's faith was so deep that she was able to turn her very existence over to God. A basic fact of the Missionaries of Charity was that it essentially operated without funds. From the beginning, Mother Teresa insisted that both her subsistence and her work would rely entirely upon Divine Providence.

Legacy

Mother Teresa wanted to do "something beautiful for God." At the time of her death in 1997, there were nearly 4,000 Missionaries of Charity Sisters established in 610 houses in 123 countries. The congregation did not cease growing with her death. Today, there are more than 5,000 Sisters. The work continues to thrive as the network of Missionaries of Charity continues to operate centers in countries throughout the world.

Although a significant number of charities and organizations bear her name, Mother Teresa never allowed fundraising to be done in her name, always relying instead on Divine Providence. Accordingly, these organizations operate without the authorization of the Missionaries of Charity (http://www.motherteresa.org/08_info/NOTIFICATION.html).

Towards the end of her life, Mother Teresa had joked that all the Sisters should die quickly because this pope was canonizing everyone. In fact, the cause for Mother Teresa's canonization was put on the "fast track" only two years after her death by Pope John Paul II, who waived the usual five-year waiting period. She was beatified in 2003. On that occasion, Pope John Paul II called her "an icon of the Good Samaritan," who chose "to be not just *the least* but to be *the servant of the least.*"

As of this writing, the cause of Mother Teresa needs an additional miracle for her sainthood. Her cause for sainthood has several websites, where interested parties can remain accurately updated: http://www.motherteresacause.info/ http://www.motherteresa.org/Novena/MadreTeresa_feast_2008.html

Prayers by Mother Teresa

Daily Prayer

Dear Jesus,

Help me to spread Thy fragrance everywhere I go.

Flood my soul with Thy spirit and love.

Penetrate and possess my whole being so utterly that all my life may only be a radiance of Thine.

Shine through me and be so in me that every soul I come in contact with may feel Thy presence in my soul.

Let them look up and see no longer me but only Jesus.

Stay with me and then I shall begin to shine as you shine, so to shine as to be a light to others.

Amen.

Nazareth Prayer for the Family

Heavenly Father,
you have given us the model of life
in the Holy Family of Nazareth.
Help us, O Loving Father,
to make our family another Nazareth
where love, peace and joy reign.
May it be deeply contemplative,
intensely eucharistic,
revived with joy.

Help us to stay together in joy
and sorrow in family prayer.
Teach us to see Jesus in the members of our families,
especially in their distressing disguise.
May the eucharistic heart of Jesus
make our hearts humble like his
and help us to carry out our family duties
in a holy way.
May we love one another
as God loves each one of us,
more and more each day,
and forgive each other's faults
as you forgive our sins.
Help us, O Loving Father,
to take whatever you give
and give whatever you take with a big smile.

Immaculate Heart of Mary,
cause of our joy, pray for us.

St. Joseph, pray for us.

Holy Guardian Angels,
be always with us,
guide and protect us.

Amen.

Anyway

People are often unreasonable, irrational, and self-centered.
Forgive them anyway.

If you are kind, people may accuse you of selfish, ulterior motives.
Be kind anyway.

If you are successful,
you will win some unfaithful friends and some genuine enemies.
Succeed anyway.

If you are honest and sincere people may deceive you.
Be honest and sincere anyway.

What you spend years creating, others could destroy overnight.
Create anyway.

If you find serenity and happiness, some may be jealous.
Be happy anyway.

The good you do today, will often be forgotten.
Do good anyway.

Give the best you have, and it will never be enough.
Give your best anyway.

In the final analysis, it is between you and God.
It was never between you and them anyway.

Made in the USA
San Bernardino, CA
18 October 2013